Beware

Beware

Jabberwocky

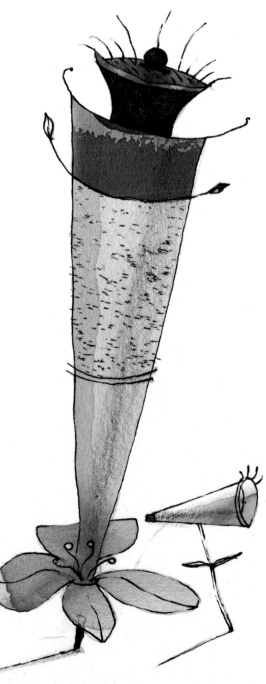

VISIONS IN POETRY

LEWIS CARROLL

Jabberwocky

WITH ILLUSTRATIONS BY STÉPHANE JORISCH

'Twas brillig, and the slithy toves
Did gyre and gimble
          in the wabe:

All mimsy were the borogoves,

And the mome raths outgrabe.

"Beware the Jabberwock, my son! The jaws that bite, the claws that catch!

Beware the **Jubjub** bird, and shun

The frumious Bandersnatch!"

He took his vorpal sword in hand:

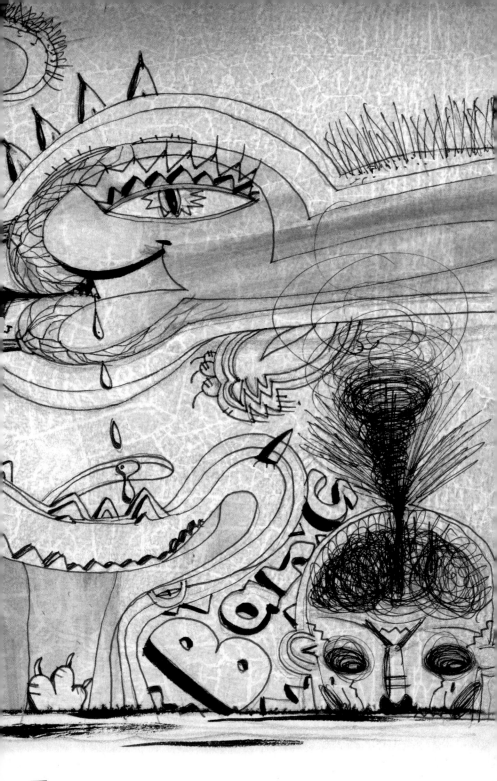

Long time the **manxome** foe he sought —

So rested he by the **Tumtum** tree,
And stood awhile in thought.

And, as in uffish thought he stood,

The Jabberwock,

with eyes of flame,

Came **whiffling** through
the tulgey wood,
And **burbled** as it came!

One, two!
One,
two!

And through
and through
The vorpal blade went

snack!

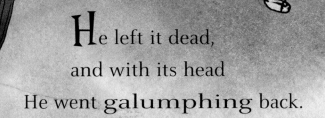

He left it dead,
and with its head
He went **galumphing** back.

"And hast thou slain the

Jabberwock?

Come to my arms, my beamish boy!

O frabjous day!

Callooh! Callay!"

He chortled in his joy.

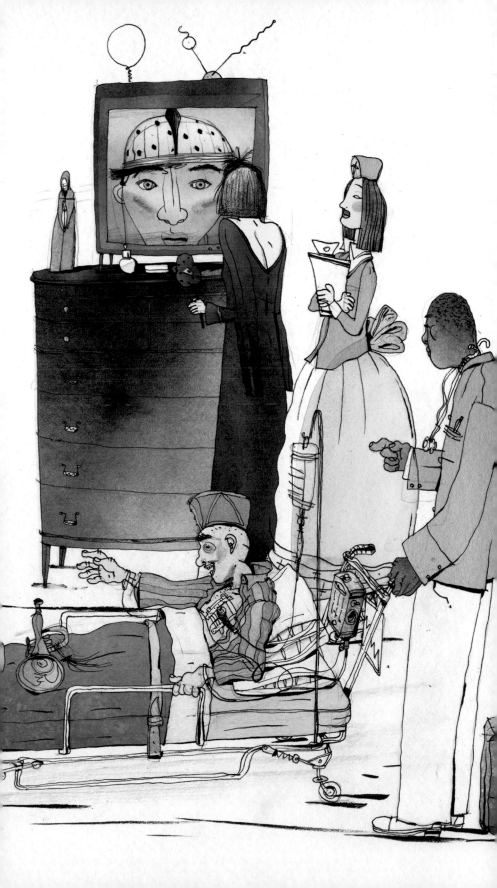

'Twas brillig, and the slithy toves
Did gyre and gimble in the wabe:

All mimsy
were the **borogoves,**

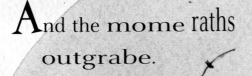

And the mome raths
outgrabe.

Lewis Carroll

Lewis Carroll (1832–98) was the pen name of the English writer, pioneer photographer and mathematician Charles Lutwidge Dodgson. Although shy, Carroll was renowned for his intelligence and wit, and cut an eccentric figure from an early age. As a child, he delighted in inventing games and puzzles and writing poems and stories for his ten siblings. He continued to pursue his love of writing and logic first as a student and later as a lecturer in mathematics at Christ Church College, Oxford. Over the course of his career, Carroll produced many mathematical treatises, but also indulged in fantastical tales and humorous verse. The most popular of these stories are *Alice's Adventures in Wonderland* and its sequel, *Through the Looking-Glass and What Alice Found There*. Both feature worlds in which logic is turned on its head, challenging readers to make sense of strange games and puzzles.

Through the Looking-Glass includes "Jabberwocky," one of the most well-known poems in the English language. Written in nonsense verse, the mock-heroic ballad exemplifies Carroll's imaginative language play. In "Jabberwocky," he created an altered sense of meaning through the coining of new words, called portmanteau words. A portmanteau is, of course, a large suitcase, and as Humpty Dumpty explains to Alice in *Through the Looking-Glass*, a portmanteau word is "two meanings packed into one word." "Chortle," the combination of "chuckle" and "snort," is one such word of Carroll's that has made its way into the English lexicon. Others, such as "slithy," the pairing of "lithe" and "slimy," remain little known beyond the context of his literary ingenuity. "Jabberwocky" continues to fascinate readers through its inventive use of language and its enigmatic lyricism, qualities that have allowed this poem to stand the test of time.

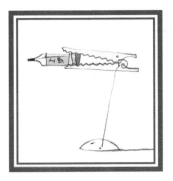

Stéphane Jorisch

Just as the nonsense words of "Jabberwocky" captivated the imagination of Carroll's heroine Alice, so do these celebrated lines conjure up many visions in the mind of illustrator Stéphane Jorisch. Taking inspiration from the poem's playful and inventive language, Jorisch's fanciful, bizarre and haunting images grew primarily out of the sound of Carroll's words. As we look through the eyes of this accomplished illustrator, what emerges is not only a tale of adventure, triumph and jubilation, but also the story of a father and a son, the old and the young, and the roles we are sometimes forced to assume by others. It is a vivid reminder that monsters come in many guises and that perception is often very different from reality. The modern, Orwellian landscape of Jorisch's vision brings this Victorian poem into the twenty-first century. A provocative commentary on contemporary media, politics, warfare, religion and gender roles, his illustrations suggest the numerous ways in which nonsense is spoken by those in authority today.

Rich, sophisticated and enigmatic, this unique interpretation of a well-loved poem serves as a springboard for the imagination. For those familiar with "Jabberwocky," Jorisch's vision brings the poem into an entirely new light. For others, it is a wonderfully compelling introduction to classic poetry. Regardless, it will open up the eyes and minds of the young and the old, just as surely as Carroll's words.

Stéphane Jorisch is the illustrator of many books for children, including *Suki's Kimono* and *Oma's Quilt*. He has received a number of honors throughout his career, including the Governor General's Award for Illustration, Canada's most prestigious literary award. In addition to his books for young people, Jorisch illustrates for magazines and has created designs for the world-famous Cirque du Soleil. He lives in Montreal with his girlfriend and their three children.

To my father and my son — S.J.

✙

The illustrations for this book were rendered in
pencil, ink, watercolor and Adobe Photoshop.

The text was set in
Celeste and DaddyO Hip

✙

KCP Poetry is an imprint of Kids Can Press

Illustrations © 2004 Stéphane Jorisch

Kids Can Press acknowledges the financial support of the Government of
Ontario, through the Ontario Media Development Corporation's Ontario Book
Initiative; the Ontario Arts Council; the Canada Council for the Arts; and
the Government of Canada, through the BPIDP, for our publishing activity.

Published in Canada by
Kids Can Press Ltd.
29 Birch Avenue
Toronto, ON M4V 1E2

Published in the U.S. by
Kids Can Press Ltd.
2250 Military Road
Tonawanda, NY 14150

www.kidscanpress.com

Edited by Tara Walker
Designed by Karen Powers

Printed and bound in Hong Kong, China, by Book Art Inc., Toronto

This book is smyth sewn casebound.

CM 04 0 9 8 7 6 5 4 3 2 1

National Library of Canada Cataloguing in Publication Data

Carroll, Lewis, 1832–1898.
Jabberwocky / Lewis Carroll ;
with illustrations by Stéphane Jorisch.

(Visions in poetry)

ISBN 1-55337-079-1

1. Nonsense-verses, English. 2. Children's poetry, English.

I. Jorisch, Stéphane II. Title. III. Series.

PR4611.J33 2004   j821'.8   C2004-900981-8

Kids Can Press is a ᴸORUS™ Entertainment company